ALIENS ARE WITH US

ALIENS ARE WITH US

❖

BILL ROUNTREE

Duncan Riley Publishing

TABLE OF CONTENTS

PREFACE

I WAS BORN in the late 1950s in Atlanta, Georgia, and grew up in a very traditional suburban lifestyle. But I had some very unusual experiences beginning at about age eight that have continued for over fifty years. I initially told my family about the experiences, but I was ridiculed, so I learned to keep quiet. Then in my teenage years, I came to learn that it was intelligent life from another planet that was visiting me, so I was even more motivated to talk to someone about my experiences. I told my friends a very small part of the story to gauge their reactions, but as expected, they also ridiculed me, so I continued to keep it all a secret as the years went on and the visits continued.

I graduated from college with a degree in management information systems, and I went on to have a successful career, eventually managing over a hundred multimillion-dollar computer software projects for Fortune 500 companies. I also had a great family, a very successful son, and great friends—everything I could want. But in the meantime, my enigmatic experiences continued, and I never told anyone else about them ... until now.

I've read that some people who make claims of having encounters with aliens are not considered credible sources because they might have ulterior motives, such as money or fame, and therefore, their claims are not considered valid. But I want to make it clear that I do not need to write this book for any possible financial gain, as I retired early with multiple houses, cars, and boats, so I am financially secure, and I am certainly not after any notoriety. Actually, it's just the opposite; I know that by writing this book, I will just open myself back up to ridicule and possible harassment. But after over fifty years of silence, it's time for me to share my experiences in depth. My story needs to be heard, and I don't want to keep it a secret any longer.

The first section of this book is titled "What I Know," because it details my experiences in which I was visited by a device averaging two or three times a year that I knew from the start was clearly not from this world. Usually, it just watched me until I did something to make it leave. But then a voice spoke to me on two occasions, revealing that they were intelligent life forms from another planet, as well as telling me some other clues as to why they are here.

The second section is titled "What I Believe," because I tell of other experiences I've had that are not cold, hard facts, like the visits I received, but instead are more open to interpretation. I also write about a few alien experiences from other very credible sources, and I share some fascinating scientific information on the possible existence of other intelligent life in the universe as well as other information about Near Death Experiences (NDE) from the new documentary film, *After Death*, and the International Association for Near-Death Studies. I conclude with several chapters on what I believe it all means, including how it all relates to the afterlife, reincarnation, and our guardian angels.

As you read my book, I believe you will agree that it is different than other books about alien encounters, because I have been visited by aliens over one hundred times spanning more than fifty years, so I have no doubt that my experiences are genuine. Aliens visiting earth are not ready to have their presence here known, so no one has all of the answers as to who they are and what they are doing here, but after over fifty years of experiences I definitely have some answers to those questions. I believe if you keep an open mind as you read and consider my experiences, along with those of other credible sources and the additional data I present, you will understand how I arrived at my conclusions and may begin to agree with many of them.

WHAT I KNOW

THEY BEGIN
WATCHING ME

WHEN I WAS seven years old, my family moved out of our small three-bedroom house and into a new, larger house in a quiet neighborhood right across the street from the elementary school. I was the baby of the family, so I got the last choice of which bedroom I wanted. My brother, being the oldest sibling, got first choice, and he chose to have the whole basement to himself. My sister chose the second-largest bedroom upstairs (my parents, of course, got the master bedroom), which left me with the smallest room. Being on the corner of the house, it at least had the advantage of an extra window. I was used to sharing a bedroom with my older brother, so I felt a little lonely in my own room, but I was looking forward to enjoying more space.

Not long after we moved in, I woke up in the middle of the night and thought I saw something in my room. It was very dark, so I could barely make out the shape of it. I sat there for a few minutes, trying to focus on it, unable to see anything conclusive— but I absolutely knew something was there. Finally, despite my fear, I jumped out of bed to try to grab it—and it seemed to just disappear.

Needless to say, I was terrified, so I ran out of my room and went to a safe place where I could sleep: downstairs in my brother's room. I went in very quietly, so as not to wake him, and curled up in the spare twin bed. Thankfully, he didn't wake up; I didn't want to have to explain myself. I lay there, still as a mouse, looking around the room to make sure there was nothing in there. His room didn't have any windows, just a bit of light from his alarm clock. I didn't see anything, and I felt safe in there with him. I finally got so tired that I dozed off.

The next morning, my brother woke me up and asked why I was in his room. I admitted that I thought I had seen something last night, and of course, he just laughed it off. Later, I told my dad what had happened, and that I wanted to start sleeping in my brother's room. He said he was fine with it, as long as my brother was too. Later that day, he told me it was okay with my brother, so I began to sleep in my brother's room. But for the rest of the day, I would hang out in my own room. It wasn't scary when it wasn't dark, so I had no problems being in there—until it was time for bed.

My brother put up with this arrangement for about a year, until he'd finally had enough. He was eleven by then, while I was only eight. Clearly, we were at different points in our development, so it was time for me to get out of his space.

One night, we were all eating dinner, and my dad began to dig into exactly why I was so scared to sleep in my own room. What had I seen? What did it look like? How many times did I think I had seen it? Why did it seem to disappear when I got out of bed? He was trying to make me understand that it was not logical to be afraid of something that didn't even seem to be real. He finally asked me to take him into my room, so we could try to see what I had seen that night.

My father and I went into my room, turned off the lights, and began to look around. "Where is it?" he asked. "Let's try to recreate what you saw." So, we sat on the edge of the bed and scanned the room. "Is that what you saw?" he asked as he pointed to a shadow on the curtain. "No, that's not it," I replied. "Well, what about that?" he said, pointing to a shadow the moon was making on the floor. "No, that's not it either," I insisted. We went through this for several minutes, with him pointing out every shadow we could see. He was clearly getting frustrated by this point, and I knew that whatever I had seen that night didn't look like anything he and I could see now. So, to appease him, I told him that maybe the shadow on the curtain might have been it. By now, I was wondering if I had really seen anything anyway, so I just agreed that that particular shadow must have been it. He remarked that the shadow looked kind of like an eagle pointing, and I laughed and agreed. So, that became the family joke for quite a while: "Billy is scared of the pointing eagle in his room."

Once I moved back into my own room, whenever I woke up in the middle of the night, I just tried my best not to look around the room, because I didn't want to see anything. I figured that if I didn't see anything, I wouldn't get scared; ignorance was bliss. I would usually pull the sheet over my head, leaving just my mouth and nose and a bit of my eyes exposed to narrow my field of vision, which was actually very comforting. That worked for a couple of years.

Then one hot summer night, I didn't have the sheet over my head, and I woke up in the middle of the night and saw something in my room again. It was in about the same spot as it had been the first time, and it was the same vague shape. It appeared to be hovering about five feet off the floor. It was only six feet away, but because it was such a dark night, I still couldn't make out what it was. I just sat there, frozen, not moving an inch as I tried to focus in on it, but it was just too dark.

After several minutes, I jumped quickly out of bed and

reached for it as I made my way towards the light switch. It was directly in my path, but as I approached, it just slowly lifted up and faded away. I flicked the light on and quickly scanned the room. Nothing. I knew better than to go back to my brother's room, or to go tell my father about it, because there was nothing there for me to show him. It must have just been the eagle pointing, I tried to reassure myself. So, I left the light on and just sat on the edge of my bed for about thirty minutes, trying to figure out what I had seen and what to do about it. Finally, I got back into bed with the light still on and just lay there with the sheet covering all but my eyes, ears, and mouth, and I continued to look in fear towards the spot in the room where I had seen the object. I eventually dozed off.

When I woke up the next morning, I didn't tell anyone. I knew it wouldn't do any good; it would just open up the barrage of teasing again. So, I kept it to myself.

The next day, when my mother and I were alone, I asked her if she could get me a night-light. I lied that sometimes it was so dark in my room that I had to fumble around to find my way to the bathroom. She said she had one I could use. I could tell she was suspicious of my reason, but she didn't ask any questions about it, just handed it to me with a smile.

From then on, I slept with the night-light on in my room. I plugged it in in a location where it would best light up the middle of the room, and I tested it before I went to bed. It did a great job of lighting up the part of the room where I had seen the object before, so I could now easily see if something was there, and I would be able to tell exactly what it was. I was more comfortable sleeping in my room now, because at least I would know for certain if something was there and be able to describe to everyone exactly what it looked like.

When I went to bed that night, even though I had the comfort of the night-light, I still tried to sleep with my eyes partially covered. But as time went on, I became a bit curious. Was there something in my room now, and if so, what was it? So, I began to not keep my eyes covered, and if I happened to wake up in the middle of the night, I would roll to my other side. I would sometimes open my eyes and look around the room, not necessarily trying to see something, but just not hiding anymore.

One night a couple of months later, I woke up sometime in the middle of the night and saw the object again—but now I was able to see it clearly, because it was lit up by the night-light. I was lying on my right side, facing out into the center of my bedroom towards the door. I lay motionless, looking at this object. It looked similar to some kind of large camera except it appeared to be floating off the ground. It was dark gray and rectangular, about one-and-a-half feet tall and two feet wide, with something round in the middle that was darker, and it had a two-piece arm that looked as if it could extend up or down. I lay in bed with my eyes open, blinking repeatedly to be sure I was focusing on it correctly, but otherwise not moving at all. I was thinking that whatever this thing was, it was not of this world.

By this time, I was only about eleven years old, but I knew enough to know that this object that was in my room, floating about five feet off the ground, was not something that could be manufactured in this world. I was never into science fiction as I grew up, but it was clear that this device had to be from another planet, because it was suspended in midair, and that is not something that can be done with our technology. I probably only lay there for four or five minutes, but it felt like a lifetime, and all of these thoughts were racing through my mind.

Finally, it was clear that it was not going to just go away, so I quickly leapt out of bed and headed towards it, reaching out my hand to grab it. As I did, it slowly lifted up and faded away, never making a sound, never changing color or shape. I went for my light switch and quickly scanned the room. Nothing was there. I was so terrified of what I had seen and scared that it was still there somewhere, so I sat at my desk with the lights on and just looked around the room. I thought about telling my family, but I knew it would just become part of the joke about the eagle pointing, so I just sat there, thinking about what I had seen and what it meant.

After about thirty minutes I got up, grabbed a pad of paper and a pencil and drew what you see below. It appeared to be a fairly simple device, but I knew that nothing about it or it being in my room was simple. I was scared and didn't know what to do. I hid the drawing between my magazines, where I knew my brother and sister wouldn't find it, and I sat awake at my desk for the rest of the night. I was scared that if I lay back down in bed, I would fall asleep—and I didn't want to fall asleep again, because it was clear that whoever had sent this device preferred to visit me while I was sleeping, and I didn't want to be visited by them again.

In those days, I focused my attention on people who were exploring our world, reading books like *Kon Tiki* and magazines like *Outdoor Life*. I didn't care about the space program that the US was pursuing, or TV shows that had to do with aliens and space travel. I just wanted to sail the seven seas, exploring the world, hunting and fishing. But here I was, being visited by some sort of device that had to be from another planet. I didn't want any part of it; I just wanted whatever it was to go away and leave me alone. I liked our world, and I was scared that whoever this was might come visit me in person—or worse yet, take me away to their

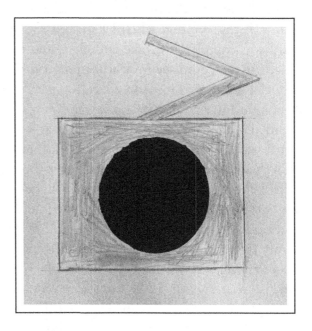

planet. And there was the fear that if I told anyone and made a lot of noise about it, the government would take me away for questioning or do studies on me. So, I quietly hoped this device would never return. I just wanted to be free to live in the world as I knew it, pursuing my own adventures on Earth. I didn't want any part of some alien universe, I just wanted to be left alone.

When it was time to get up, I left my room and went through my usual morning routine. I ate breakfast with the family and didn't say anything about what I had seen in my room last night, because I knew it was pointless. I knew that I couldn't explain it, and that I wasn't even sure if I believed it myself, because it made no sense. I had seen alien movies and shows like *The Twilight Zone* that had a lot of other-worldly themes, but even as a kid, I had never believed any of that was real. It was just science fiction or fantasy, pure entertainment, just like the mummy and the werewolf and the rest of it. I was sure that when I had seen the object in my room, I was completely awake and alert, and there was enough light that I could see it clearly enough to draw the picture. But maybe it was just some kind of crazy dream in which I thought I was awake. So, I just went on with my life and pretended it hadn't happened. Maybe it was just a fluke. Whatever it was, I didn't want it to be real, so I just buried my head in the sand and tried my best to forget about it. But you'd better believe I still slept with my night-light on.

About two months later, I woke up in the middle of the night, and there it was again—the same object in the same spot, silently facing me. At this point, the only explanation was that something was watching me. Or maybe whoever it was could also read my mind, like I had seen on movies and in TV shows; that definitely creeped me out. I just did the same thing, remaining completely still and blinking my eyes to focus on it as best I could, trying to make sure that what I was seeing was really there and that I was wide awake. Part of the reason I didn't move was that I was petrified, and being a child, I stupidly thought that if I didn't move, it would just go away. I was also scared that whoever was controlling this thing would appear before me, maybe take me away to some-place else. I liked my house, my family, my friends, and my neighborhood; I didn't want to leave and didn't want any of it to change.

This time I waited a bit longer before I made any move-ments, probably about ten minutes total. Instead of jumping up and running for it, I just sat up in bed and kept watching it for a few minutes more. It didn't move or change in any way; there was absolutely no indication from the device that it cared that I had moved, or that it had even seen me move. Finally, I had had enough and jumped out of bed, reaching for it as I made my way to the light switch. As it had in the past, it just slowly lifted up and faded away, but quickly enough that it was gone before I could reach it. I went to my desk and sat there with the light on, looking around to make sure it was gone. After about thirty minutes, I went back to bed, but left the light on. I hoped that would keep it from coming back that night. I drifted off to sleep and eventually woke up when my alarm went off, glad that I had not seen it again.

That day when I went to school, I asked my best friend if he had ever seen anything in his room in the middle of the night. I didn't want to say that I had, but I wanted to find out what he thought about something like that before I told him about my experiences.

"What, like a ghost?" he said in a sarcastic tone.

"No, I don't know... Just something weird," I replied vaguely.

"No," he said, even more emphatically. "I don't have ghosts walking around in my room. Why, do you think *you* see ghosts?" He chuckled.

"No, of course not."

"Then why did you ask about it?"

"Oh, I just saw a movie about things like that," I said. "I just wondered if it ever really happens."

"No, that's just a bunch of crap. Ghosts aren't real. What, do you believe in werewolves too?" he asked, still chuckling.

"Of course not. Forget it, it was just a weird movie," I replied. I quickly changed the subject, and I didn't bring it up again with anyone. I knew it was just too far-fetched for people to believe, and I still didn't know what to make of it myself, or how to explain what I had seen or what I thought it might be, so how could I expect anyone else to believe it?

THEY FIRST SPEAK TO ME AND TELL ME WHO THEY ARE

O VER THE NEXT few years, I kept my night-light on and pulled the sheets up over my head with just my mouth and nose and a bit of my eyes exposed, because I didn't want to see that device watching me. I kept hoping that whoever was visiting me was done with me and would now leave me alone. Other than their infrequent visits, I had a completely normal middle-class life in suburbia. I went to the elementary school right across from our house, I was in the band, I had lots of friends, I was in Cub Scouts, and I had two great parents. My dad was an attorney, and my mom stayed home with us kids. I was more adventurous than my siblings and dreamed of sailing the seven seas, camping, fishing, and other outdoor adventures. I was totally uninterested in science fiction, aliens, and UFOs. I just wanted them to leave me alone so I could live my nice, normal life.

But they didn't. I continued to wake up during the middle of the night several times a year, and I would see that same object watching me. I knew that since I typically didn't look for it and only saw it two or three times a year, it was undoubtedly there much more often than that, but I didn't ever want to see it, so I continued to try not to look around the room in the middle of the night.

Over time, I became slightly less afraid of it—but I was still scared that they might appear in front of me, or take me away, or do something physical to me. So, I just lay still in my bed, watching it, and hoped it would disappear on its own—but it never did until I got out of bed and reached for it. Then it would always just slowly fade away. Since I had become somewhat used to it, I would often flick on the light for a few minutes, look around the room to make sure it was gone, then just turn off the light and get back in bed.

When I was fourteen, I woke up in the middle of night and saw the object watching me as usual. I just stayed perfectly still as I looked at it, hoping that at some point it would go away on its own. But instead, after only about one minute of me looking it, they began to speak.

When I heard them speaking, I was initially terrified, because they were escalating their interaction with me. But I was so accustomed to lying still as they watched me that I didn't move as they spoke; I just lay there, perfectly still. I was scared about what might come next, but the voice was soothing and calm, so I just listened. It was a man's voice, unremarkable and with no accent, and while he was speaking at a slightly slower pace, he spoke with authority. It seemed to be coming from inside me, so I naturally had no worry about anyone else in the house hearing him, because I could tell it must be a telepathic connection.

After a few seconds, the man's voice finished what it was saying, and for the first time ever, the device left without me reaching for it; it just faded away. After it was gone, I got up, turned on the light, and got back in bed, pulling the covers up to my neck. Now I no longer had any doubt as to who "they" were, and I understood that all of these years of them visiting me could not be explained away as someone from Earth traveling back in time, or someone from Earth visiting me from a different dimension, or someone from Earth having invented this device that could appear and disappear on command. The object watching me was clearly something created by aliens from another world.

I was really scared now about what might happen next, but I didn't know what to do about it. No one had ever believed me in the past, and I had no reason to think they would now, so I felt like it would do no good to tell anyone. But I knew what I had seen for these past five years or so, and I knew what I had heard them say that night. This hadn't been some random one-time dream, but that wouldn't matter to anyone I might tell; it was too hard to believe. I got up and wrote down exactly what they said:

"You humans have come a long way since we left you on the beach thousands of years ago."

I hid it in a book, along with the drawing I had made of their device, and stayed awake all night with the lights on. I was terrified of what might come next.

As I sat there, I began to wonder, why had they picked me? Surely there were other people around the world whom they were watching and speaking to—but how did they pick whom they would interact with, and again, why me? Maybe our house was just a random house they stopped by, and when they came into my room, I didn't totally freak out when I saw them watching me, so they kept coming back. They undoubtedly knew I was becoming less scared of them, so maybe that was why they chose to speak to me and tell me who they were. But why had they told me that? What did they want me to do with that information?

Then again, maybe I hadn't been selected at random. If they had these kinds of capabilities, who knows—maybe they could travel into the future or were able to see into the future, and they knew I needed to know this information.

Maybe I was going to be someone important in the future. Or maybe I was going to have children who were going to be someone important in the future, and they would need to know about the aliens and why they're here. But I knew I wasn't going to tell anyone about this now. They wouldn't believe me—and if they did, and it got out, the government might come for me and take me away for observation and experimentation. Again, who knows? I just knew I didn't want any part of it. I just wanted to live my life and to be left alone.

Over the next few years, they continued to visit me two or three times a year on average. It was always the same: I could see their device clearly, thanks to the night-light, and it would just hover and watch me. I usually waited about ten minutes before I got up and reached for it—no longer in a mad dash, just slowly getting out of bed and walking towards it as I reached for it, and it would slowly fade away. Afterwards, I would usually just get back in bed, turn onto my other side, and pull the sheet up over my head, with only my nose and mouth and a bit of my eyes exposed, and go back to sleep. It was becoming a common occurrence. I was still scared whenever they visited, but I became so used to it that I wasn't terrified any longer. I just didn't want them to visit in person, or worse yet, take me away to someplace else, or escalate their interaction with me in any way.

One Saturday at about 8:30 in the morning, when I was seventeen, I was lying in bed with my hands behind my head, thinking about what I was going to do that day. Some friends and I were going to look at cars (one of our favorite things to do), and I was thinking about going out for some breakfast before I met up with them. As I lay there, I glanced to the right—and there it was! This was the first time I had seen it in broad daylight. It looked pretty much the same as it did at night: a dark gray case with a black round object in the center that appeared to be a lens. I sat there and looked at it for a few minutes, and this time it just slowly disappeared without me getting up and reaching for it. It was a bit disconcerting, because they seemed to be getting bolder. I hoped that wouldn't be a trend.

THE FIRST
PHYSICAL VISIT

ONE NIGHT SEVERAL months later, I was sleeping alone in the house, and I had my most disturbing experience yet. By this time, I was a senior in high school, both my brother and sister were away at college, and my parents had divorced. My dad was living elsewhere, and my mom had remarried with someone living in another state, so she was often away with him, as she was on this particular night. I was awoken in the middle of the night by a noise that sounded like something was being dragged across my bedsheets. I immediately tried to get up—but I could not move at all. Each time I attempted to move my limbs or my head, or even open my eyes, I felt something similar to an electric shock that was keeping me from moving, except there was no pain. All I felt when I attempted any movement was a shock-like vibration, but I kept fighting it because it made no sense to me, so I couldn't understand why I couldn't overcome it.

Eventually, I would stop resisting for a minute or two and felt no sensation at all, but then I would try to move again, and the vibrating force would return and keep me completely restrained. I'm not sure how long this went on, but all of a sudden I was able to move, and I instantly jumped out of bed and turned my lights on. There was nothing in my room, and I had no lingering sensations from the incident, but needless to say, I was really freaked out.

I sat on the edge of the bed for quite a while, trying to

make sense of it all. I supposed that it could have been the product of some strange sleep state that I was in. But my inability to make any movements at all, even just opening my eyes, combined with the sound of something like a strap being dragged across the bed, led me to the conclusion that it must have been the aliens visiting me. For some reason, they needed to touch me. Maybe it was some test they were doing on me. I wasn't sure, but it was too bizarre of an experience to have any other explanation than alien contact. It was about three in the morning when I first got out of bed, but I was too scared to go back to sleep for fear of them coming back, so I stayed up the rest of the night. Eventually, I went out to the family room and turned on the TV. The chairs facing the TV were in the middle of the room, but I was still so scared that I turned all the lights on and kept looking behind me to make sure I was alone. It was a very frightening experience.

A few days later, I was with my three best friends, and we were driving around aimlessly, as we often did in those days. None of us ever had any alcohol or marijuana or anything else; we just drove around, listening to music and talking. Occasionally we would drive by a friend's house and see if they were home, or go to a convenience store and get sodas, or just park in a parking lot somewhere and talk, which is what we were doing. I had known them all since elementary school, and we talked about everything, so I thought I would very lightly broach the subject of my latest experience. I wasn't going to tell them any specifics, but I wanted to see if they would possibly be open to some discussion about it and see where it went.

"I had the weirdest experience the other night," I began. "I woke up at about three in the morning, but I wasn't able to move; I couldn't even open my eyes. Any time I attempted to move, it was like a force was holding me still. Have any of you ever had anything like that happen to you?"

"Oh, yeah, that's happened to me before," Mike said as he looked towards the other guys with a slight smirk on his face. "Hasn't that happened to you before, Brent?"

"Oh, sure, sure," Brent replied. "That just happened to me about a week ago." He attempted to hold back his grin and began nodding his head towards Jim. "How about you, Jim? Hasn't that happened to you?"

They were all looking back and forth at each other as they smirked, so I knew this was going nowhere. I needed to just attempt to back out of it before it got out of hand. "Ha ha, very funny," I said. "Okay, I guess it was just some weird dream, then. It just seemed bizarre, so I thought I would bring it up. Come on, let's get out of here." I started up the car. "There's nothing going on here. Where do guys want to go now?"

I began pulling out of the parking lot, so the subject instantly changed, and it was never brought up again. It was just another confirmation that I couldn't tell anyone about my experiences; they were just too different and unbelievable. It was clear that without irrefutable evidence or someone else to witness what was going on with me, I would not be able to discuss it with anyone. It was going to have to be my secret, something I kept totally to myself. I knew aliens existed, because what I'd experienced just could not be done with our current technologies, not to mention what they'd said to me. I just wanted them to stop visiting me.

They didn't. Over the next year, I had at least two more visits from them in which they just watched me. I say "at least" because those were the ones that I woke up for. They could have been watching me many more times or for longer durations than I was aware of, and I just didn't wake up. I didn't believe they just watched me though; they were clearly able to communicate telepathically, which to me meant they were able to read my thoughts, and therefore, they might have been monitoring me in more ways than I was aware of. I often wondered why they were monitoring me, and I began to think it might be an experiment to see how humans would react to knowing that aliens exist, and how we would react to the information they shared with me about their involvement on Earth.

About a year after my first physical visit, it happened again. This time I didn't hear the distinct noise that sounded like something being dragged across the sheets. Instead, I heard another odd noise and immediately woke up, but when I tried to open my eyes to see what it was or make any movement, I was again held in place by the same mysterious force. Any movement I attempted was stopped by the same feeling, like a shock without pain, just an odd vibrating feeling. I knew I couldn't move or open my eyes, so I just stopped fighting it and lay there waiting, trying every minute or so to move, just continually testing my abilities. I didn't feel anything touching my body or hear anything at all; I just wasn't able to move. I should have begun counting or doing something to help me keep track of the time or understand what was going on, but I didn't. I just lay there, attempting to move every so often.

I wasn't sure when it had started or how long it lasted, but at some point I was able to move again, so I abruptly jumped out of bed and turned on the light. I looked over my body—just my arms and legs and torso, as I was in my underwear—and I didn't see any physical markings on me. So, I just sat down on the edge of the bed and tried to recall anything that would help to understand what had happened, but I was not able to think of anything that helped me figure out the details. I was too terrified to go back to sleep, fearing that they might return, and that they might even be watching me now as I sat there, so I stayed up for the rest of the night. I began to read *Kon Tiki* again to try to get my mind off of what had just happened, and I continued to read until the sun came up. Then I began my day, going about it as usual, like nothing had happened. Per usual, I didn't say a word to anyone about it.

LIVING WITH
THEIR VISITS

W HEN I WAS a senior in high school, I was not too sure what I wanted to do about college or a career, so I procrastinated on applying anywhere. But two of my closest friends had applied early to the University of Georgia and were accepted, and they made plans for rooming together. Another one of my close friends had a good job in Atlanta and planned on continuing to work there as he went to school. I just worked at a sandwich shop, and I didn't have that kind of option, so I finally decided to apply to Georgia and just take my chances with a roommate—if I even got accepted, of course, especially considering that I was applying so late.

I got my acceptance that summer and started college in the fall. Since I was the youngest child in the family and therefore the last to go to college, my parents were no longer into the ritual of taking me to school and helping me get situated in my dorm. So, I just drove myself to Athens, Georgia, where the university is located, and checked into my dorm building. I'll never forget walking down the hall (it was just cinder block walls for dorms in those days) and hearing some very loud, freaky music playing. (This was in the '70s, and I listened to mainstream rock music, but this was something I had never heard before—and didn't particularly want to hear again.) The closer I got to my dorm room, I realized that yes, this godawful noise was coming from my new room.

The door was open, and there was my roommate, lying on his bed, with hair halfway down his back (I was the clean-cut type). He looked up at me standing there with my suitcases in my hands and then just laid his head back down without saying a word. I put down my luggage and walked over to my friends' dorm, telling them about the roommate I got stuck with.

After a few weeks, it was clear that my start at college life was not going too well. My roommate and I never clicked at all. My friends at Georgia included me in some of their fun, but since I didn't live close by, I often missed out on it. I really didn't even want to be at Georgia, since I had no clue what I wanted to major in. I would often talk to my friend in Atlanta, and things there sounded as fun as it had been when we were in high school. So, after about a month, I withdrew from college and went back to my parents' house in Atlanta. My parents were living elsewhere at the time, and my brother and sister were both off at college, so I had the whole house to myself.

Not long after I moved back home, my visits from the aliens continued at about the same rate, every three or four months. I hadn't seen them while I was in my dorm at Georgia, but of course, they may have visited and I just wasn't aware of it. So, I wasn't sure if their visits were location-specific, and they just came to this house I lived in, or if they somehow followed me. Time would tell.

About a year later, my two friends had also left the University of Georgia, and we decided to all get a four-bedroom apartment together in Atlanta, along with my friend who had stayed there. About two months after we moved in, I awoke in the middle of the night to a familiar sight: the camera-like device was watching me. I didn't have my trusty night-light in the apartment yet, but I had a private bathroom and slept with its light on and the door cracked, because I never wanted to sleep in a room that was completely dark. I lay still in bed, watching it for a while, wondering how they were able to find me in a new location like this. Had they possibly implanted some sort of tracking device in my body when they physically visited me? Or since they could clearly read my thoughts, maybe they were able to locate me with some device that could detect my unique brain wave patterns, much like fingerprints. I imagined that would be possible, since they clearly have very advanced capabilities. Locating me amongst the millions of other people in Atlanta—or for that matter, the billions of other people in the world—seemed like a daunting task, but maybe it was simple for them.

I continued to look at the device, waiting to see if it would eventually leave, or if they would talk to me again, or if something different might happen. I was as scared as always, but no longer terrified like I used to be. I had certainly grown accustomed to their presence, and by now, I didn't think they were going to take me away or do anything harmful to me. Of course, I could never be completely sure, so I remained somewhat frightened of them. After about ten minutes, I wanted it to go away so I could go back to sleep, so I did what I had become accustomed to doing: I quickly got out of bed and walked towards it, reaching out for it. As I did, it slowly lifted up, as if it were retracting, and then it faded away. I knew that just because I could no longer see it didn't necessarily mean it was truly gone, but it was more comforting to not have to look at it, and I hoped that meant they had left me. I immediately got back into bed and turned on my side to face the other direction, pulled the bedding up over my head with just my eyes, nose, and mouth exposed. I continued to think about how they had been able to find me in a new location, until I fell back asleep. The next day when I was with my friends, I acted like I always did—like nothing unusual had happened, and life was normal, and everything was straightforward and easily explained, as we had been taught.

The apartment arrangement didn't last long, so about six months later, I was back at my parents' house, which was always an easy fallback since no one lived there. Aliens continued to visit me from time to time while I was there, still averaging about two or three times a year, and they would just watch me in the same way they always did. After about a year, I went back to the University of Georgia and joined the fraternity my two best friends had joined, and I moved into the fraternity house. The house had about thirty guys living in it. I shared a room with my two friends, and while I was there, I never saw them visit me. I thought maybe if there was someone else in the room, then they wouldn't visit me. I wasn't sure, but it was nice not to have that always hanging over my head. I always looked for them when I woke up in the middle of the night for any reason, but it was comforting to not see them watching me, and to feel like they would not come if others were in the room with me. Ideally, they were through with me and would never visit me again.

The following year, I got married and moved into an apartment with my wife while we were both still students at Georgia. I was hopeful that they would not visit me anymore, since I was now sharing a bed with her. But after about six months, I awoke for some reason and looked over and saw the camera-like device watching me —or this time, watching us. I lay in bed looking at it, and it just stayed in place, facing right towards us. After a few minutes, I decided to see if my wife could see the device too. I started nudging her gently, but she just mumbled and continued to sleep. So,

I coughed loudly while pushing her more forcefully, and this time she woke up, a bit angry. "What?! What are you doing? Why did you push me?" But as soon as she woke up and spoke, the device just faded away. "Sorry," I said, "I must have been dreaming." But now I knew they were not done with me, and that they would continue to visit me even when I wasn't alone, but they wouldn't let someone else see them. It would have to remain my secret.

I was originally a biology major because that had been my favorite subject in high school. But after I got married, I got serious about school, and I knew biology wouldn't get me much of a job, so I changed my major to premed. I was really obsessed with turning my grades around and getting into med school, so I made straight A's every semester for about two years. But my friends had already graduated from college, and I was not happy with the thought of another year of it, followed by med school and an internship. Plus, I knew what a huge commitment being a doctor would be, and I knew that wasn't really what I wanted to do with my life. I wanted to travel the world, sailing, exploring, and having fun. So, I went to the career counseling center at Georgia to find out what other options I might have.

The counselor looked over my grades and told me that if I kept it up, I would definitely get into a good med school, but he warned me that it was a long and expensive process. I'll never forget him pulling out a newspaper from the stack of papers on his desk and saying, "Look at these jobs. If I were in your shoes and had your aptitude for math and science, this is what I would do. See this job? With only two years of experience, they're paying forty thousand dollars a year for a programmer!" This was in 1982, so I knew about programming and computer science, but it was still a fairly new field, so I had not really considered it. After I left his office, I did more research and talked it over with my wife, who was certainly all for it. So, I decided to change my major and take twenty hours of classes a semester, so I could finish college in just a year and a half. Computer science suited me better anyway. It was somewhat fun and somewhat creative, it paid well, and it was very flexible, which would allow me opportunities for more fun and adventures.

My wife graduated from Georgia, so we moved back to Atlanta so she could start her new job, and I transferred to Georgia State to finish my degree. We got an apartment, and I finished school in less than two years and got a good job offer in Chattanooga, Tennessee, with National Cash Register (NCR) as a systems engineer. During our two years in Atlanta, there had only been one other time when I woke up and saw them watching me. I always kept a night-light in our bedroom, and I explained it by saying that I needed it for when I got up in the middle of the night to go to the bathroom. On that particular night, I woke up and was going to go to the bathroom when I saw the camera-like device in the corner of our room. I watched it for about five minutes and decided not to try to wake my wife, so I just got up and headed towards it, and it faded away. That was the only time I noticed it, which was a longer absence than in the past, but it is very likely that there were other times they came to watch me, and I just didn't happen to wake up and see it.

Over the next thirty years, I continued to see the alien device on a fairly regular basis, still about two or three times a year. My personal life continued on a pretty standard path for someone with a degree in computer science who also had some people skills. After two years working for NCR, I moved back to Atlanta and went to work for Price Waterhouse as a management consultant in their information systems division, and I traveled around the east coast for various projects. During my time traveling and staying in hotel rooms, I never saw the device watching me, but I did while I was at home.

My marriage to my first wife ended when I moved to Chattanooga for my first job, but I remarried in 1988 to a very intelligent woman who was a teacher. We had a son in 1990, so I quit my job with Price Waterhouse because of all of the travel, so that I could stay home more with my wife and son. I soon got a job in the R&D division at American Software. She and I divorced in 1994, but during my time with her, the aliens visited several times a year. Some of the times I saw them, I would try to wake her up by slowly and quietly talking to her while I gently nudged her, hoping that if I did it quietly, they would not leave. But every time she began to wake, they would fade away.

I eventually got to the point where sometimes when I woke and saw the device, I would just roll over, facing away from it, and go back to sleep. I didn't like them watching me, but I had grown so accustomed to it, so that depending on my mood, I just didn't really care anymore. Other times, if I was waking up because I needed to go to the bathroom, I would watch it for a few minutes, then get out of bed and walk toward it, reaching for the device, so that it would just do its thing and fade away.

I stayed on at American Software, working various roles, including as a designer and architect. Then in 1998, I became a project manager, managing projects for major clients such as Sprint PCS, Harley Davidson, Porsche Cars North America, and many others. The projects I managed were decent-sized projects with up to fifteen or twenty direct reports, with a budget of up to five million dollars. I traveled around the country and sometimes overseas, leading meetings with the various teams. By now, I had owned and lived in some lakefront houses and beachfront condominiums, and I bought a forty-foot sailboat and had owned many smaller racing sailboats. I had lifelong friends I often hung out with. My son was a very bright student, and we had a great relationship. But all the while, I had my alien visitors checking in on me on a regular basis. I continued to keep it a secret, because I knew from experience how it would be received by everyone, and at this stage in my life, considering the career implications, it would not have been a wise decision to go public with it. So, as usual, I kept it to myself.

The aliens continued to watch me at the various houses I lived in, and with the different women I had long-term relationships with, sometimes even visiting me at my girlfriend's house. I would occasionally try to wake her, but every time she began to wake up and speak, they would fade away. I felt like that was one of the reasons they continued to watch me; I didn't get freaked out and scream and panic, I just lay there and let them observe me. Undoubtedly, they were reading my mind whether I was awake or asleep, and maybe even doing scans of my body. There's no telling what else they were doing, but it certainly seemed like they were observing me as part of an experiment or an analysis of the human race. I was sure I wasn't the only one that aliens were interacting with, but I continued to try to ignore it as best as I could and just enjoy my life. I did buy one book that was popular during those years that was about someone being abducted by aliens. I read part of it, but it was too troubling for me to read the entire book. One of my fears was being abducted like he was, and the small part that I read was terrifying to me, so I didn't want to read any more of it. Living with their visits and knowing that what they'd told me was enough for me. I didn't feel the need to learn more about aliens and didn't want to immerse myself in that world, so I just tried my best to ignore it.

In my twenties and beyond, I didn't experience any more visits that I felt with a hundred percent certainty had a physical component, like the two I'd had as a teenager. But there were certainly other experiences in which I believed aliens were involved; those are discussed in the next section, "My Experiences that I Believe Had Alien Involvement."

THEY SPEAK TO
ME AGAIN

T HE NEXT TIME they spoke to me, it was a very cryptic message, and I'm still trying to understand why they said what they said and what the underlying meaning was, but maybe I will know for certain in time.

The year was 2016, and I had just moved to California and was visiting my son at the house he was renting. He had graduated from college in 2012 and moved to Southern California for a job, and he told me he loved it there and was never leaving. He and I are very close, so I began thinking that with him living on the other side of the country, I would only see him a few times a year. He is the most important person in my life, so seeing him so infrequently was just not acceptable. After he graduated from college and got his job, it became clear that he would not be coming back to the house we had lived in in Atlanta for twenty years, so I sold it and bought a place in Cocoa Beach, Florida. I was dating a woman who was going to stay with me in Cocoa Beach half the time and at her house in Atlanta the other half, but she ended up not doing that, so I began to think about moving to California too. I still had a forty-foot sailboat, so I thought it would be cool to move it to Southern California, live on the boat, get some cool car like a Ferrari, and get a job somewhere north of Los Angeles. After all, it wasn't working out with the woman I was dating, and I was ready for a change. I talked to her about moving out there with me, but she wouldn't commit, so I packed up my boat and had it shipped across the country to Los Angeles.

I drove my car across the country with my personal items and got to my son's house at about 6:00 p.m. We had dinner and made it an early night because he had to be up for work very early the next morning. I was staying in his office on an air mattress, and I slept in until about 9:00 a.m., got up to go to the bathroom, then sat down on the sofa and began looking at my phone. When I looked up, there was the camera-like device, facing me. The room was well lit by the sun shining through the window, so it was completely visible. I looked at it calmly for about a minute, and then I heard a voice say:

"Now that you are living in California, we will not visit you again."

I couldn't help it; I simply thought, *Good*, because I was tired of them visiting me. I just sat there, continuing to look at it, and after just a few seconds, it lifted up as if it were retracting and slowly faded away. I immediately began puzzling over what their message meant. It was fairly cryptic, so there were many possibilities. My first thought was that maybe it was about my safety, because the east coast was going to be hit by nuclear bombs or a terrorist attack, and I would be safe here in California. Then I thought maybe it wasn't about me at all; maybe it was to somehow help my son. Maybe me being near him in California would save him from something, or maybe my support would help him with some part of his life. Time would tell what their statement meant, but the more I thought about it, the more likely it seemed that by me moving to California, I was making a commitment to stay with my son and support him, so they were saying they no longer needed to visit me because I was now doing what they wanted me to do.

Over the next few years, I had some other experiences that gave me clues as to what their statement meant, but it is more conjecture than fact. What I do know without a doubt is that they visited me again and spoke to me, and that it was going to take time for me to fully understand why they said what they did.

WHAT I BELIEVE

MY EXPERIENCES THAT I BELIEVE HAD ALIEN INVOLVEMENT

A FTER ALL OF the experiences I've had throughout my life, which convinced me beyond a shadow of a doubt that humans are not alone here, that aliens were involved in our creation, and that they continue to be involved in our lives, I now look at the experiences that I and others have had in a different way. Given that so many people around the world have had things happen to them that can't be explained logically, I think back to what a woman I worked with while at NCR said about a software issue I was having: "There's got to be a logical explanation!" Very true.

PHYSICAL EXPERIENCES

We've all heard many, many accounts of people that have been in dangerous or life-threatening situations, but were saved by what they believe was some type of divine intervention. For example, maybe they were pinned beneath a car that was about to explode into flames, and someone came and lifted the car off of them, but then vanished, and no one recalled seeing the mysterious stranger. People that have been saved often believe without a doubt that they were saved by God or an angel, because there was no way a mortal human would have been able to save them. Of course, the "experts" and skeptics explain it all away with some logical theory, because you can't put in the police report that the person was saved by God or an angel, or because some people are just natural skeptics, and it's far easier and more acceptable to be a skeptic and point to the logical explanation than it is to believe something that is not widely accepted and can't be supported by known facts. But when you are actually one of those people whose life has been saved during what is usually a fatal event, then you often believe differently than the skeptics or those who try to explain away the unexplainable. You believe you were spared due to some type of unexplained intervention.

I went through one such incident when I was in my early twenties, which to me is further evidence that we are not going through our lives alone, like other animals that roam the earth. A friend and I had gone out to get something to eat, but it was not a drinking kind of night, so we each only had one or at most two light beers. We both weighed about two hundred pounds, so we were certainly not legally intoxicated, but I suppose today they might call it "driving buzzed." It was the mid-seventies, and I was driving a 1965 Mustang Fastback—certainly a car I wish I still had today, but they were very common back then. Very few people wore seatbelts at the time, so we were driving without one on. We were only going about fifty miles an hour, which was about the speed limit, and it was out in a sparsely populated part of Atlanta, so we were the only car on the road. We were listening to the radio, talking and laughing, and my friend played around like he would occasionally do back then, grabbing the steering wheel and swerving us back and forth slightly on the road.

I'm not sure what happened next—whether I grabbed it back and jerked too hard, or if he accidentally swerved too far. But the right front wheel came off the pavement, and apparently there was a not insignificant drop-off alongside the road. So, the steering wheel spun out of control, and the car quickly came to a right angle to the road and began turning onto its side. The car flipped over and over and over, ending up upside down, half on the road and half off. But the entire time it was rolling over, I felt as if I were in a bubble. It was very surreal, as I wasn't banging around inside the car; it felt more like I was floating. My body was rolling with the car, but it wasn't touching any part of the car at all as it rolled over and over. My friend later told me he felt exactly the same way in that moment.

When it stopped flipping, we both asked each other if we were alright, which we were, and then we kicked the doors open to get out. Neither of us had any broken bones, no concussions, not even a bruise. My friend did have a minor scratch on his forehead, but it didn't even require stiches. We walked about a mile to a restaurant and called the police. When they arrived, they looked at the car, and the officer told me that based on the point where it started flipping, the speed we were going, and the damage to the car, he estimated it had rolled three times. The car was almost flattened. It was a terrifying sight to see. He said the last time he'd seen a car like that, both occupants were dead on arrival, and that it was a miracle that neither of us had been injured.

I know skeptics will say that centrifugal force pinned us to the top of the car and kept us from being hurt, and it happens all the time, etc. But they were not in the car and didn't feel the sense of being in a protective bubble. I will never forget it—and I'll always believe an "angel" was watching over us.

In November of 2020, I had some other strange experiences that I couldn't explain. But when all the pieces are put together, along with my other life experiences that I've accepted as fact, the logical explanation is that an alien physically visited me. But because I didn't see the device watching me or actually see an alien, I put it in this section with "what I believe."

This event occurred during the middle of the COVID-19 lockdowns, and since I could no longer go into the office, I left my apartment in Sacramento and moved to my house in the mountains of California, where I worked remotely as an IT project manager. About two feet of fresh powder snow had fallen in the last twenty-four hours, but around midnight, the snow had stopped. I had just gotten up to go to the bathroom, but got back in bed because it was very early in the morning, and the skies outside were just beginning to lose the pitch-black darkness, so I hoped I would be able to fall back asleep before the sun came up.

My house is chalet-style, and my bedroom is on the second floor, so the roof is right over my head. Thus, the noises that I then began hearing on the roof were so close to me that they were frightening—and they continued for a full twenty minutes. I was convinced that the only way those noises could be made was by something walking on the roof. Now, I've slept in that room about half the time over the four years that I've owned the house, and since it's in the mountains outside of Tahoe, there is usually snow on the roof five months out of the year. I've heard the sounds of snow settling and sliding on my roof many, many times through the years. But these noises were completely different, so I was terrified.

I stayed completely still, with the covers pulled up as usual, with only my mouth, nose, and a bit of my eyes exposed. I knew it was completely absurd to attempt to hide from them, because if it was aliens on my roof, then they certainly knew I was there. But I was terrified that this time, they might appear to me in a face-to-face encounter—or even worse, they might abduct me, because it has always been an inanimate object watching me, not a physical being. Needless to say, it was a very scary experience.

I was so sure that someone was on my roof that I also considered skiers, hikers, or snowboarders. My house is on a hill, and the snow packs up on the hill behind the house, so skiers have been known to ski over the top as if it were a ramp. But since it was mostly dark outside, I knew that was very unlikely. Another explanation that I also deemed unlikely was that it was an animal of some sort. But whatever was on my roof was much heavier than a squirrel or even a fox, and the bears were all hibernating at that time of year, so the most likely explanation to me continued to be that it was an alien. I stayed there quietly and made no movements, just hoping they would go away but was truly terrified, more so than I had been since my first physical visit more than forty years ago. Finally, the noises stopped, but I lay awake for another hour or so until it was fully light out, then got bundled up and went outside to see if I could find any clues.

I walked outside to find a beautiful blanket of deep, fluffy powder snow covering my yard and the woods behind me. I've seen many tracks in the snow through the years, like mice or squirrels moving from the base of one tree to another, birds walking through portions of the snow, or coyotes, foxes, or even bobcats coming down from the woods behind my house and circling it, looking for something to eat. But that day I saw some very odd tracks that I have never seen before or since, and I couldn't come up with a logical explanation.

They were certainly not your typical animal tracks. One particularly disturbing aspect of the tracks was that they started (or stopped) in the middle of the yard—not at the base of a tree, not coming down from the woods, but right in the middle of the yard, where they continued about thirty feet to the edge of my house. The snow in the woods surrounding my was still perfect, not disturbed by the wind blowing chunks of snow off the branches, and no melting, dripping, or refreezing had occurred. It was a perfect untouched blanket of snow, so I was easily able to distinguish the outlines of the tracks. These were not like any manmade tracks at all, but more like very narrow skis or snowshoes. They were only about two inches wide and fourteen inches long, but some were a bit longer, which of course could be due to sliding around in the snow. I thought about what kind of animal could possibly have done this, and the only thing I could think of was if a mouse dug up from underneath the snow and walked in a straight line for about fourteen inches, then either jumped from the end of one to the beginning of another, or dug back under the snow and popped up to begin the next. I'm sure you will agree, a mouse doing that for thirty feet—and matching a bipedal walking pattern—is completely absurd.

Since we are in the age of cell phones, I took pictures and videos and showed them to a friend who is a bona fide mountain man. He's been living in the mountains for over fifty years and is also a big hunter, and he offered what he acknowledged was a very unlikely explanation about a bird of prey dragging a mouse randomly through the snow, but then said realistically nothing he knows of could have made those tracks in the snow, "except perhaps an alien." This was astounding, because he knows nothing about my experiences or this book I've been working on. So, based on my previous experiences and knowledge, an alien visiting me was the most logical explanation. Of course, as far as my digital "evidence" goes, just about anything nowadays can be faked, and skeptics can always come up with alternate explanations. But again, if they had lived through my experiences, they would not be skeptics.

POSSIBLE VISITS WHILE I WAS SLEEPING

I feel that any experiences I have when I'm sleeping are in a different category than those I have while fully awake, because dreams can certainly be very bizarre. But there have been a couple that are significant and which I suspect had some outside influence, or which were actually experiences involving aliens that happened while I was asleep.

One night a couple of weeks after the incident where I saw the tracks in the snow, I was asleep, and I don't recall having any particular dream at that moment. But I suddenly felt an upward motion, and I was rotating slowly as I moved upwards. I looked down and saw Earth fading away beneath me. The next thing I recall, Earth was coming into focus beneath me again, but this time I was moving towards it, and I was dropped quickly down. Instantly, I was completely awake in my bed. I immediately sat straight up, but I felt extremely dizzy, so I steadied myself by putting my arms out to my sides to hold myself upright. I sat there for a few seconds, thinking through what had just happened, but the dizziness was really bothering me, so I lay back down, continuing to try to make sense of what I had just experienced. Within a few minutes, the dizziness had passed. But I was a bit scared, trying to think back on what I had seen and felt to try to determine whether I might have really just left Earth and returned. I wasn't terrified like the other times when they were watching me or walking around on the roof above me, because this time it was in a dream, and it may have been nothing more than a dream but the feelings I had during the dream combined with the bizarre dizziness made me think that something may have actually occurred. I was sixty four years old at the time and had never, ever had an experience like this before so it seemed very unlikely it was just a dream.

I was also wondering why they would continue to visit me at all, because in 2016, they said they would not be visiting me anymore now that I'd moved to California. It's true that I have not seen their camera-like device visiting me again, so maybe that's what they meant? Or maybe it was different aliens that visited me using that device for all those years? Either way, I had hoped it was over, so now I was back to wondering what might be next and no longer knowing what to expect.

About a month later, in January of 2021, I had an unusual dream that was very memorable. In my more than fifty years of having these visits from aliens, other than the possible dream about leaving Earth, I have never dreamed about aliens or anything that is not a normal part of the world we live in. Typically, when I do have a dream that is odd for some other reason, I wake up in the middle of the night and think through the dream and plan on remembering it, so I can tell someone about it—but by the time I wake up the next morning, the full memory of it is gone. I've talked to others about similar incidents, and it seems that is how dreams work; it's unusual to remember them beyond a certain period of time. This dream, however, is one that is vividly branded in my memory. It wasn't a long dream or very involved, but the image was significant, and I will never forget it.

My second wife was a very loving, kind, and caring person, and also very intelligent. We had a son together, but for various reasons, our marriage did not last. She passed away when our son was eleven, but I always loved and cared for her. That's the way I am with most people in my life that I love; I don't stop loving them just because we are no longer together. But with her, it was different; she was in a separate category. Maybe it was because we had a son together, but I definitely loved her more than other women I had relationships with. That night, I don't recall thinking about her for any reason, but I had a dream in which she came to visit me. There was no particular action or theme to the dream; she just came to visit. The unusual part of it was that I only saw part of her face. I only knew it was her because of her eyes, which were very distinctive. I could not make out the rest of her face. Her eyes had the loving, contented look that you see in the eyes of some people. You don't need to see their whole face; you can look into their eyes and see the emotion they are experiencing, and hers was definitely a kind, loving expression. I woke up immediately after the dream ended and was not scared at all, but content and pleased with the thought that it seemed her soul and even her connection with me lived on in a different form. I didn't get up to write any of this down because I felt confident that it was something I would remember forever, and I have.

OTHER RELIABLE
REPORTED UFO AND
ALIEN EXPERIENCES

I'VE NEVER BEEN overly interested in reading about the space program or aliens, because I've had enough real-world experiences with aliens and spent enough time living in that world, so reading about and researching them was not something I typically enjoyed. But when I finally decided to write this book, I did some research, and what follows are accounts of some experiences from very credible sources that I found very compelling, and I believe they are worth sharing.

UNITED STATES MILITARY INVESTIGATIONS THROUGH 1969

In 1947, the US Air Force began Project Sign to determine whether UFOs were a threat to national security, and to scientifically analyze the data on UFO sightings. The initial findings from the project were written up in 1948, and they concluded that flying saucers were real phenomena, were not made by the United States or the Soviet Union, and were likely extraterrestrial in origin. This conclusion was rejected by USAF Chief of Staff General Vandenberg, who stated that there was insufficient physical proof, and he then dismantled Project Sign.

At the end of 1948, Project Grudge was initiated by the US Air Force, and many believed that its mandate was to debunk the UFO sightings that had been reported. It concluded that all the UFO sightings were either natural phenomena or otherwise mistakenly identified, but it did state that twenty-three percent of the sightings could not be explained.

Several influential US Air Force generals were dissatisfied with the UFO investigations under Project Grudge, so in March of 1952, Project Blue Book began. It continued to investigate UFOs, but it in the latter years it was believed that very few serious investigations were being done, and it too had become more of a means of debunking UFO sightings. In 1969, Project Blue Book was closed. A recorded total of 12,618 sightings had been reported to the project, and of those, 701 remained "unidentified" in spite of the intense scrutiny that was given to discredit them.

UFO EXPERIENCES AND SIGHTINGS BY ASTRONAUT GORDON COOPER

Gordon Cooper was an American astronaut, and as such, he was a very credible source who believed UFOs were visiting Earth and needed to be investigated by the US government. He was an aerospace engineer, test pilot, USAF pilot, and one of the seven original astronauts selected for Project Mercury. In 1963, he piloted the longest and final Mercury spaceflight, Mercury Atlas 9. He also became the first astronaut to make a second orbital flight when he commanded the Gemini 5 mission in 1965.

Cooper stated that he saw his first UFO while flying over West Germany in 1951, and that he had seen others several times during his career, so he felt compelled to investigate the possible existence of UFOs more deeply. So, in May of 1957, he asked James Bittick and Jack Gettys, who were part of the team at Edwards Air Force Base, to set up an Askania Cinetheodolite precision landing system in an area on the base. This Cinetheodolite system was able take pictures at thirty frames per second when aircraft landed. They set up both still and motion picture cameras, and when Gordon returned later that morning, they stated that they had seen a "strange-looking, saucer-like" aircraft land there and later take off. They stated that the strange aircraft hovered over them, then landed about 150 feet away, and then took off again as they got closer to the craft. During these maneuvers, the craft didn't make any sound. Cooper stated that both Bittick and Gettys were very experienced in working with various aircraft that were being tested on the base, but both were very unsettled by what they saw.

Cooper had been given a number at the Pentagon that

was to be used to report unusual incidents, so he called them, and they instructed him to develop the film and send it to the Pentagon in a locked courier bag. Cooper had not been told not to look at the negatives, so he did, and he reported that what he saw in them was exactly what Bittick and Gettys had reported to him. Since an unidentified aircraft had landed at a classified military base, Cooper expected the Air Force to conduct further investigations into the incident, but he never heard anything about it and never saw the photographs again.

UFO ACTIVITY RELATED TO US NUCLEAR MISSILE SITES

In 2022, the US announced the creation of the All-domain Anomaly Resolution Office (AARO) within the Office of the Undersecretary of Defense for Intelligence and Security. It expanded and renamed the Airborne Object Identification and Management Synchronization Group (AOIMSG) by adding submerged and transmedium objects to their scope.

A defense.gov press release stated, "The mission of the AARO will be to synchronize efforts across the Department of Defense, and with other U.S. federal departments and agencies, to detect, identify and attribute objects of interest in, on or near military installations, operating areas, training areas, special use airspace and other areas of interest, and, as necessary, to mitigate any associated threats to safety of operations and national security. This includes anomalous, unidentified space, airborne, submerged and transmedium objects."[1]

Robert Salas, a retired US Air Force captain and former intercontinental ballistic missile launch officer, testified to the AARO about an incident that had occurred in 1967, when he was heading up the Malmstrom base in Montana. He and other members of his base saw eight orange lights that they identified as UFOs over the base, and at the same

---

1. "DoD Announces the Establishment of the All-domain Anomaly Resolution Office," U.S. Department of Defense, July 20, 2022, https://www.defense.gov/News/Releases/Release/Article/3100053/dod-announces-the-establishment-of-the-all-domain-anomaly-resoluti on-office/.

time, warning lights began to go off, indicating that the ten nuclear missiles at his base had been disabled. It was reportedly never investigated, and the staff on site at the time of the incident had to later sign documents that they would not divulge information about the incident.

Another incident involving UFO interference in US military operations over fifty years ago was also investigated by the AARO. In 1964, Robert Jacobs, also a former US Air Force officer, was filming a test missile launch when a saucer-shaped object fired beams of light at the warhead of the missile that was being tested, which caused it to fall out of the sky and crash.

US MILITARY AND COMMERCIAL PILOTS AND UAPS

Former US Navy lieutenant and F-18 pilot Ryan Graves is a co-founder of Americans for Safe Aerospace, and he is one of the two US Navy pilots that testified before congress in July of 2023 about the threat that Unidentified Aerial Phenomena (UAP, formerly referred to as UFOs) pose to those operating in US airspace and to the security of the United States.

Graves stated that he and other Navy pilots have regularly witnessed UAPs—so much so that discussing them had become part of their preflight briefing. He stated that UAPs fly in such a way that they defy the laws of physics as we know it, exhibiting flight characteristics and performing maneuvers that are not possible with the aircraft known today. One incident he reported involved a UAP that was approximately five to fifteen feet in diameter that came towards two F-18s and flew between them at a high speed, which of course was a very dangerous maneuver, and as such, it should have been investigated—but he knows of no official acknowledgment of the incident.

He also stated that over thirty witnesses had come forward to report UAP incidents, and many are commercial pilots with decades of experience. They have no way to report UAPs except by contacting law enforcement, and many are concerned that making such reports might impact their employment.

STATEMENTS FROM ISRAELI'S FORMER DIRECTOR OF SPACE PROGRAMS

Haim Eshed is a retired brigadier general in Israeli military intelligence, and he was the director of space programs for the Israeli Ministry of Defense for nearly thirty years, as well as a visiting professor of aeronautics and astronautics at various space research institutions. In 2020, he made headlines by saying that people on Earth had been in contact with extraterrestrials from a "galactic federation." He also told Israel's *Yediot Aharonot* newspaper that "The Unidentified Flying Objects have asked not to publish that they are here, humanity is not ready yet." He went on to say that they were equally curious about humans and are seeking to understand "the fabric of the universe," and that "there is an agreement between the U.S. government and the aliens. They signed a contract with them to do experiments here." He also said President Trump had been in touch with the aliens, and they did not want him to reveal their existence because it could trigger mass hysteria.

I personally am not surprised by any of the above statements, and if they are true, they would certainly help to explain why the US and other governments don't appear to be thoroughly investigating UFO claims, or at least not revealing their findings. But when Eshed went on to say there was a joint base on Mars that is shared between US astronauts and aliens, that seemed a bit far-fetched to me, because of the magnitude of the cover-up that would be required. However, Eshed was highly respected as the head of Israel's space program and has spoken about the existence of aliens for decades, so perhaps he knows more than people give him credit for, and the government naysayers are just part of the cover-up.

SCIENTIFIC STATEMENTS CONCERNING OTHER INTELLIGENT LIFE

THERE ARE CERTAINLY varying opinions about whether there is other intelligent life in the universe, but while researching for this book, I came across a fascinating article that to me further supports what I've experienced regarding the existence of other intelligent life in the universe. It discusses recent discoveries concerning exoplanets (planets outside our solar system), in which scientists now believe that roughly one-fifth of the stars in the universe have planets that are in the "habitable zone" that could potentially support life. Scientists estimate that there are 2×10^{22} stars in the universe, which is two hundred billion trillion stars (or to write it out in the standard notation, that's 200,000, 000,000,000,000,000,000). That's a lot of stars! And if the new estimate is that one-fifth of the stars in the universe have at least one habitable planet, that's 4×10^{21} stars or 40 billion trillion stars with at least one habitable planet. These estimates seem to be continually evolving, but even if you knock off a few zeroes, it's still an extremely high number.

The article discusses a paper that was published that applies this new information to an equation, called the Drake equation, which is used to estimate the number of active, communicative extraterrestrial civilizations in the Milky Way galaxy.

"The question of whether advanced civilizations exist elsewhere in the universe has always been vexed with three large uncertainties in the Drake equation," said Adam Frank, professor of physics and astronomy at the University of Rochester and co-author of the paper. "We've known for a long time approximately how many stars exist. We didn't know how many of those stars had planets that could potentially harbor life, how often life might evolve and lead to intelligent beings, and how long any civilizations might last before becoming extinct."

By applying the new exoplanet data to the universe's 2 x 10 to the 22nd power stars, Frank and Sullivan find that human civilization is likely to be unique in the cosmos only if the odds of a civilization developing on a habitable planet are less than about one in 10 billion trillion, or one part in 10 to the 22nd power.

"One in 10 billion trillion is incredibly small," says Frank. "To me, this implies that other intelligent, technology-producing species very likely have evolved before us. Think of it this way. Before our result, you'd be considered a pessimist if you imagined the probability of evolving a civilization on a habitable planet were, say, one in a trillion. But even that guess, one chance in a trillion, implies that what has happened here on Earth with humanity has in fact happened about 10 billion other times over cosmic history!"[2]

It's easy to read the above paragraph and just gloss over the numbers, but those are really amazing numbers, because the universe is so vast and has so many stars. It's truly mind boggling. So, he states that given the estimated number of habitable planets in the universe, if only one in a trillion (which are very small odds, given one trillion is 1,000,000,000,000) of those planets that are habitable developed intelligent life, then there would be ten billion (yes, 10,000,000,000) other planets that have developed intelligent life in the universe!

The article goes on to discuss some other factors that may limit other intelligent life from interacting with us, such as how long they might be able to survive on their planet and the distance they are from us, making it difficult (or impossible) for communication or travel between the two planets. But if you look at how far we have come on Earth in just the last hundred years, it's not hard to imagine us having a permanent station on another planet in fifty years, one that is mostly self-sustaining in another hundred years, and one that is completely self-sustaining and well populated in a thousand years. So, to me, the ability for us or other intelligent life to continue to thrive as life forms is not really constrained by the planet we are currently on—or may be living on in the future—being able to sustain life long-term. As for the question of other intelligent life being able to visit us or communicate with us, Einstein stated that nothing can travel faster than the speed of light, so if that is true these stars that are forty or more light-years away would essentially be too far for communication or travel, provided it uses technology we can understand today. But scientists have theorized about the ability to exceed the speed of light, and that if it were

---

2. Leonor Sierra, "Are we alone in the universe? Revisiting the Drake equation," NASA, May 19, 2016, https://exoplanets.nasa.gov/news/1350/are-we-alone-in-the-universe-revisiting-the-drake-equation/.

possible, it would imply time travel. So, to me it's possible for aliens to travel here or communicate with us, just not with our current technical knowledge and capabilities.

WHAT I BELIEVE IT
ALL MEANS

ALIENS ARE WITH US

BASED ON MY experiences alone, I know that aliens are visiting us here on Earth. And if you include data from scientists about the probability of the existence of other intelligent life in the universe, plus the hundreds of thousands of reports of sightings and contact from people all over the world (and many of those are from very credible sources), it's easy for me to accept that aliens are visiting us on a regular basis and have been for many years, if not thousands of years. If I had only been visited a few times, or if the visits had always been in the middle of the night, I would not be so confident that they were genuine visits from aliens. But after over one hundred visits spanning more than fifty years, and sometimes in broad daylight, I have no doubt that they were genuine. The only object I have ever seen in my life that was not an ordinary object in our world is that device that has come and monitored me. I've certainly never had any hallucinations or been a drug user (besides marijuana very rarely) or a heavy drinker, and I've never been prescribed any drugs or medications at all besides the occasional anti-biotic for sinus infections so there would be no reason at all that these visits I experienced were something that I imagined and not genuine. Whatever this device was, it definitely is not something that we have the technological capability to create—especially since they first began visiting me in the mid-1960s. I've considered many possibilities about this device visiting me, such as maybe it was humans visiting from our future, or from an alternate universe, but it makes no sense that they would lie to me by implying that they were not human.

While doing research for this book I attempted to find some current data on UFO and alien sightings or encounters as well as statistics on investigations that have been done on these encounters. There are several organizations that people can report their sightings to but I found very little in the way of data on thorough investigations that have been done. Therefore in the absence of good recent data I've created a probabilistic argument (which uses probability and logic in uncertain situations) to estimate these numbers and based the root numbers on the data collected from Project Blue Book since it seems to contain the most thorough data that has been analyzed on alien encounters.

If we revisit the data from Project Blue Book and update the scope to get the full picture of the number of sightings that realistically have occurred worldwide, the numbers get very interesting. From 1947 to 1969, there were 12,618 sightings reported to the US Air Force Project Blue Book team out of which 701 remained 'unidentified' in spite of the intense scrutiny given to debunk them. But those were just sightings that occurred in the United States, and we only make up about six percent of the world's population, so if the number of sightings was gathered worldwide, it could potentially be over sixteen times that. Additionally, those are just the sightings that were reported to Project Blue Book, but there are many, many more people like me who have been keeping quiet about their sightings and experiences because they don't want to be ridiculed, harassed, or possibly have their job security impacted. So, I would say that very, very conservatively, only thirty percent of the sightings or contact with aliens that occur would actually be reported to something like Project Blue book. And lastly the world's population has more than doubled since those years so that also needs to be factored in. So, if you do the math, we would have the results below. I facetiously named it the 'Rountree equation' but then again thought why not formalize it because it might help to bring some attention to the number of alien encounters happening worldwide.

Rountree equation—estimated number of alien sightings or encounters per year worldwide:

$N = Pt / Ft / Fr * Pi / Pn$
$N = 12,618 / .06 / .3 * 2.7 / 22$

$N = 86,031$

Rountree equation—estimated number of 'unidentified' alien sightings or encounters per year worldwide:

$Nu = Pu / Ft / Fr * Pi / Pn$
$Nu = 701 / .06 / .3 * 2.7 / 22$

$Nu = 4,779$

where

N = estimated number of alien sightings or encounters per year worldwide

or Nu = estimated number of 'unidentified' alien sightings or encounters per year worldwide and

Pt = total number of Project Blue Book (PBB) encounters

or Pu = number of 'unidentified' PBB encounters

Ft = the fraction US population is of world total

Fr = the fraction of sightings reported to PBB

Pi = population increase since PBB

Pn = number of years PBB data was collected

EARLY HUMAN INVOLVEMENT WITH ALIENS

The aliens who visited me made the statement about leaving humans on the beach thousands of years ago when I was fourteen years old, so I was still relatively young and didn't think too much about the implications of that statement. I mostly have a math and science type of brain, so I have always been fairly logical about things. Add to that that I didn't go to church very often when I was growing up, so I didn't have strong faith in any religion, and I never truly believed that there was a God who created the universe and everything in it. It just didn't make sense to me that there would be an entity like that. After all, where did God come from? How did God get these powers? Where does God reside? There were just too many holes in that story, and basically, it just wasn't logical to me. At the time, I just believed humans had evolved like the other animals, but we turned out smarter than them and have opposable thumbs that are capable of manipulating objects easily, so we can work with tools. Now I believe differently, but at the time, that was my opinion.

Over the next ten years, as I began to take more courses in science in both high school and college, my opinion began to change. I was originally a biology major in college and took courses in things such as evolutionary biology, and by then, I had learned more about the evolution of man and basic genetics. At the time, the concept of the "missing link" was still talked about, and I began to think that the missing link was related to what the aliens were referring to when they said, "We left you on the beach thousands of years ago." I believed then—and still do—that the aliens filled in the gap of the missing link. I believe the aliens themselves are not capable of surviving on Earth, either because our gravity is too weak or too strong, or our air is not compatible with what their bodies require, or the environment here is too harsh for them on a long-term basis for a host of other reasons. So, to establish intelligent life on Earth, they genetically modified primates or early humanoids, possibly by using some of their genetic information, but maybe just by engineering them to have increased intelligence and other factors to enable them to thrive. Some people state that it would not be physically possible for them to mix their genetic material with ours, which may be true with our current capabilities, but the aliens are undoubtedly so much more advanced than we are that we can't truly conceive of what is possible for them and what's not.

"ANGELS", REINCARNATION, AND THE AFTERLIFE

When the aliens told me in 2016 that "Now that you are living in California, we will not visit you again," I was unsure of what they were trying to tell me. At first, I thought it meant that I would no longer be in physical danger from some sort of catastrophe, but now that it has been seven years and both my son and I have left California, I believe it was the other alternative I seriously considered: because now that I had moved to California I would be there to support my son. Looking back on the enigmatic visit I believe I had from my late former wife (the mother of my son) in 2019, I have come to believe that after she passed away in 2001, her soul or consciousness and memories took another form, and perhaps she was involved in the visit I had from them in 2016, because she would have wanted our son to have my support from me living close by. This all leads me to believe our souls are connected through our different lives and through the years, and that some of the "angels" that watch over us are actually the other souls we are connected to. Furthermore, because of what the aliens said to me in 2016, I believe that they are somehow involved in the way souls pass through time and migrate to other bodies and other forms. It certainly sounds far-fetched based on what we know today, but if you consider how far humans have come in the last hundred years and imagine where we could be in a thousand years, fifty thousand years, or even a million years, it certainly allows you to consider a nearly infinite number of possibilities.

When I take what I know to be true—that aliens were the ones that created humans or assisted in our creation—and what I believe based on experiences I have had and other factors discussed below, which is that they are concerned with our well-being, it's logical to extrapolate further and conclude that they also are in fact the physical "angels" involved in unexplained life-saving events because only they would have the capability to perform these 'miracles.'

When I was in my early twenties, I had an experience that first made me seriously consider the possibility that reincarnation exists. I often had an odd feeling that I had been hung up by my heels in the distant past, as if in a prisoner-of-war type of situation. It was just a passing feeling that I occasionally had when I was lying down on a bed, but I didn't think too much about it and mostly just ignored the feeling. One day, I was in between school and work and had an urge to get in my car and head out west. My family had gone to the Grand Canyon when I was about ten, but I had never been to Colorado and beyond or to the northwest. I was living alone in my parents' house in Atlanta at the time, because they had divorced and both remarried, so I just left a note saying I was heading to the northwest and would be back soon, in case someone came looking for me. I didn't tell my friends about it because I didn't want to answer all the questions about what I was doing or why, as I didn't have a good explanation, plus I felt sure I'd be back within a week.

So, I loaded my car up with some camping gear and my dog and headed northwest. This was before the days of cell phones and GPS, so I just used a map and decided to head towards Montana, because I had read about it in books about Lewis and Clarke and other outdoor adventure stories, and it sounded like a cool place to go. On the afternoon of the second day, I was driving through Nebraska and saw a sign for Grand Island, and completely spontaneously, I just took the exit and began to head towards it. I took a couple of random turns and saw a sign for a community park of some type, so I headed towards that. When I got there, I walked over to a display that had some information about soldiers from that area who had died during World War II. I read the details of one specific soldier, a marine in the Pacific who had died while he was a prisoner of war. I suddenly started crying, got back in my car, and headed straight back home.

Through the years I have heard stories of reincarnation in which the researchers state that some children have very strong and distinct memories of a previous life, and that these memories are very strong while the child is very young but then begin to fade as they age. There was one particular case that I recalled hearing, about a young boy that had some detailed recollections about being a fighter pilot in World War II. I found an article in NPR from January 5, 2014 in which Rachel Martin was interviewing Jim Tucker, a professor of psychiatry and neurobehavioral sciences at the University of Virginia, who had researched many cases regarding reincarnation for his book *Return To Life,* including this particular case of a boy named James Leninger.

When James was two years old he often had nightmares about being in a plane crash, but then during the day he would tell his parents that he had been a pilot and had flown off a boat but his plane was shot down by the Japanese. He recalled the name of the boat and that he had been killed in Iwo Jima and even remembered the name of a friend he had on the boat. After several years of research James's dad was able to verify the information that James had shared including the name of the aircraft carrier and the name of the friend that James said he had on the boat. This led to finding the name of the pilot that had died during a battle in Iwo Jima whose plane had crashed just like James had described it, with this friend whose name James recalled flying in a plane right next to him as it happened.

The boy, James, lived in Louisiana and the fighter pilot that died in World War II was from Pennsylvania. Plus the fighter pilot had been killed fifty years before James had these recollections so it's extremely unlikely that James or anyone he or his parents knew could have come across this information by normal means which gives even more credibility to this being an amazing example of someone being reincarnated.

My personal experience with my trip to Nebraska certainly offers no proof at all of reincarnation, but it was very strange and something I never told anyone about because they would not understand. It's one of those things that you have experience yourself to truly understand.

The belief in reincarnation can be found all the way back to the first century BC. The ancient Celtic peoples, including the Gauls and Druids, believed that people's souls would enter into another body after they died, as did the German tribes and the Greeks, and even Plato spoke of reincarnation around 400 BC. Reincarnation is a major belief in Buddhism, Hinduism, and Sikhism, and references to it appear as far back as 1100 to 500 BC. The basic belief is that you if accumulate good karma and lead a virtuous, moral life, you will have a more favorable reincarnation in your next life, but if you do not live a good, moral, virtuous life, you will be "downgraded" in your next life.

There are thousands of people that have openly discussed their past-life experiences on television, in books, and in other media that caused them to believe in reincarnation, and there are literally billions of people worldwide that already believe in it. It's hard to believe that billions of people are wrong.

While reading an article about a new documentary film, *After Death*, I came across some interesting information about Near Death Experiences (NDE) which further supports my belief in the existence of an afterlife.

"According to the data presented, of those who have had an NDE, a full 23 percent of them described themselves as 'visiting Hell'. On the flipside, the handful of other interviewees describe their experiences as transcendental and cleansing. They all claim to have seen their deceased bodies from above before departing for high skies, and looking down at stunning and expansive celestial landscapes while being completely devoid of fear, doubt, pain, or apprehension.

All were told that their time on earth was not done and that they would have to return. So pleasant and awakening was his journey that car crash victim Don Piper exhibits marked levels of resentment, because he was shown the way to the Promised Land only to be forced to return to life on earth.

In what is the most telling and hard-to-dismiss example, brain surgery patient Pam Reynolds (via archival video) describes watching her lifeless body on the operating table while identifying music playing in the operating room and specific medical instruments used by attending personnel.

Prior to the surgery, Reynolds (now deceased) was put into an induced coma and had her body temperature lowered to 50 degrees in order to prevent shock during the operation. It would have been impossible for her to recall any details of her operation, as she was clinically dead at the time."[3]

To me, this information ties in with the philosophy that your soul keeps reincarnating into a different form over and over again until you get it all figured out and live a totally virtuous and moral life. Many religions also purport that your soul doesn't immediately transfer from one body into another; there are different realms of existence that your soul can be transferred to.

Reincarnation, the afterlife, and angels are very controversial subjects and are difficult for many people to believe, because many are looking for physical evidence they can see and touch. I certainly never believed in any of these metaphysical concepts when I was young, but through the years as I have experienced some of it myself, and heard and read thousands of stories about them, and also have various connections to these concepts through my experiences with aliens, I now believe all three are part of our journey through life. We've all heard and read stories about people recalling their past lives, sometimes in details that they shouldn't know. There are also countless stories about people who have died on the operating table or in an automobile accident, but minutes later, they came back to life, and they speak of the other world that they witnessed after death. Then there are the stories I mentioned earlier about "angels" that had superhuman strength and lifted a car off someone on the side of the road after an accident, but then disappeared. There have been so many of these stories that I just can't fathom that these people were all just imagining what they describe.

I continue to go back to the same stance that I have regarding UFO sightings and alien contact. That is when

---

3. Michael Clark, "After Death: What's on the Other Side," Epoch Times, October 27, 2023, https://www.theepochtimes.com/bright/after-death-whats-on-the-other-side-5516584.

so many people, undoubtedly millions of people around the world, and many of them totally credible, put their reputation on the line and open themselves up to ridicule, job loss, or worse by coming forward and sharing these types of experiences then what they are stating must be genuine experiences. Yes, a small percentage of these people may have other motives or be imagining something, but so many do not. They just want to share their beliefs, concerns, and amazement regarding what they have experienced.

RELIGION AND ALIENS

I was born into a Christian family and went to Sunday school and church for a brief period when I was young, but I've never been a firm believer in any particular religion. As I got older, I learned more about many different religions and began to think that the truth is probably a mix of them. To me, it always seemed naïve to assume that the specific beliefs your religion teaches are correct, and the other four to six billion people in the world are somehow wrong. But I do believe that many of the prophets, apostles, and others that are discussed in the texts of the different religions may very well have existed, and many of the incidents that have been documented as part of their belief systems quite possibly could have happened. But based on my experiences, I believe the logical explanation for divine inspiration, visits from angels or deities, or an individual doing something normal humans cannot do is that aliens were instrumental in what occurred, using capabilities that only they possess.

Christians believe in one God, and one of the main events in Christianity is the crucifixion of Jesus. Many historians agree that parts of the event can be verified through writings from many sources, including ancient Roman writings. The resurrection of Jesus, however, is something that many skeptics do not believe actually happened, but I am of the opinion that something that is documented in so many sources and believed by so many people may have really occurred. But instead of God bringing Jesus back to life, I feel it is more logical to believe that aliens that were involved with humans' existence on Earth were the ones most likely to have brought him back to life, because with their advanced technological capabilities, that could very well be possible.

Additionally, many people have long believed that the scriptures in the Bible are a collaboration between humans and God, but I believe the humans got their inspiration from the aliens, through some sort of direct contact and they were the source of the collaboration.

Muslims believe in one all-knowing God, Allah, and that several prophets were sent to teach Allah's law, including some of the same prophets that Jews and Christians follow, such as Jesus, Abraham, Moses, and Noah. But Muslims believe that Muhammad was the final prophet, and he was sent by Allah to reveal their faith to mankind. Islamic writings say that archangel Gabriel visited Muhammad and ordered him to recite the words of Allah, and that Muhammad continued to receive revelations from Gabriel for the rest of his life, which were the basis of the Quran. Again, I believe the divine inspiration for the prophets was actually the aliens that have been instrumental in the lives of humans for thousands of years or more.

The followers of Judaism also believe in one God who revealed himself through prophets, including Abraham, Jacob, Moses, Solomon, and others. The Jewish sacred text is the Tanakh. The first five books of the Tanakh are called the Torah, which are the same as the first five books of the Old Testament in the Christian Bible. Jewish people believe that God first revealed himself to a Hebrew man named Abraham, who became known as the founder of Judaism. Again, I believe the prophets received their inspiration from aliens.

Buddhism and Hinduism are very different from Christianity, Islam, and Judaism in that they do not recognize a single creator deity, but instead offer a number of different deities. Buddhism rose out of Hinduism, and they both preach reincarnation and that living a moral and honorable life will lead to salvation and enlightenment. As with the other religions, I believe that the multiple "deities" they recognize were guided and inspired by aliens.

I wanted to go through the specifics of some of the more widely practiced religions in the world to show what I believe are some common threads and similarities. You could just say replace the word "God" with "aliens," but it's not quite as simple as that. I believe that aliens that were very invested in and involved with our planet and the human race were the inspiration for the various religions around the world. They either inspired the humans that became prophets and deities, or some of these prophets and deities could even be of alien origin themselves. Then they went on to create the sacred texts and spread the word through various monks and other religious leaders, so that people around the world would follow the teachings in the religious scripts and lead more moral and honorable lives. To further inspire and motivate the general population, the aliens would certainly have had the capability to perform miraculous feats that ordinary humans could not, such as possibly raising Jesus from the dead, or even enabling Moses to part the Red Sea so his followers would have safe passage.

I believe that with all humans sharing a common origin and having the same entities responsible for the creation of the various religions, there is a deep bond between us all that is not realized in today's different religions, cultures, and societies. I also believe that we share another common bond in that our souls are all on the same journey through existence. But there are many different phases in the development of a soul, so we might feel as if we are different from one another, but in reality, our souls are just at different phases in their development.

WHY GOVERNMENTS WILL NOT REVEAL WHAT THEY KNOW

Based on my experiences, I've long believed that many of the alleged crashes of alien aircraft and the various UFO sightings by military pilots, astronauts, and others that have been documented for the last eighty-plus years are most likely factual incidents, and as such, the government denying them is part of the cover-up of alien activity in the US and around the world. I've also felt for many years that it is natural that the US and other foreign governments that have knowledge of these activities would need to conceal it from the general public. If the governments around the world acknowledged that intelligent life from other planets exists and has been visiting Earth for decades—or more likely, hundreds or thousands of years—there would be mass hysteria. It would be such a huge shift in the way billions of people around the world think that there would be utter chaos.

There are billions of people on Earth who are deeply religious, and learning that intelligent alien life forms exist and have been visiting Earth for untold years would cause many of them to question their faith, drastically changing the way they see the world and live their lives. Billions of people around the world would stop supporting the churches, synagogues, mosques, and other places of worship, which would cause organized religions around the world to collapse. With their collapse, the many organizations, schools, and charities that they support would also collapse, and many people would be displaced and lose their direction in life.

Other reactions to this news would include people being fearful that the aliens have sinister motives, or that the aliens would be considered by some to be the new leaders of Earth, here to create a new world order, which would only add to the chaos. This is certainly not something that the existing world governments want to happen which is clearly another reason for them to be motivated to cover it up. Additionally, billions of people around the world would be insisting that the governments reach out to the aliens to ask them to provide assistance to the people of Earth with technological advances that could help humans. Corporations, politicians, and others would believe that humans could stop development and focus on alternative energy sources, medicines, new methods of producing food, and other major initiatives, with the belief that the aliens could supply those capabilities and advancements to us. But it's very likely that much of the advanced technology the aliens have could not be reproduced by humans, let alone maintained moving forward.

Some existing conspiracy theories regarding alien activity on Earth are that governments may be hiding their knowledge of aliens and the technology they have received from them, because if some new technology—such as the ability to create free energy—were released into the world, it would bankrupt many large, wealthy corporations around the world and cause economic turmoil. Another theory is that some countries do have alien vessels that they have recovered, and they are attempting to reverse engineer their technology to give their countries an unbeatable advantage with new military weapons, so naturally they would not want to reveal this information.

Regardless of whether the conspiracy theories about intelligent life from other planets visiting Earth are true or not, there are many completely understandable and valid reasons why governments may be withholding information that would confirm their existence. Releasing new facts about aliens would clearly cause mass hysteria and social and economic disruption worldwide. But governments are going to need to reveal what they know sooner than later, due to the number of credible sources coming forward about their experiences; in particular, those involving the military cannot be ignored. Revealing the information slowly would undoubtedly be the best approach, and it appears that is exactly what they are currently doing.

WHAT WE CAN EXPECT FROM THE ALIENS

I believe we can and should expect nothing from the aliens, at least in the next few years to a few decades. When governments around the world finally reveal that aliens exist and are indeed visiting Earth, they will make announcements and slowly release more and more details, but they will undoubtedly not propose any changes in the short term, to help minimize the panic and fear. Eventually, they would trickle out some new technology, and I'm sure there are some ways the aliens could help us improve our lives by advancing some of our capabilities, such as showing us how to modify our crops to grow faster or not need fertilizers or insecticides, and sharing with us about different medicines we can make to treat or eliminate diseases. But more drastic changes or those that use new technology outside of our current capabilities would take time to develop and implement.

Realistically, some alien technology that might be extremely useful to us—for example, generating energy that is clean and inexpensive—would probably be very difficult if not impossible for us to recreate with our existing capabilities and resources. The equipment they use, the materials or elements needed for that equipment, the elements that provide their energy (if they even exist on Earth), and the skills people would need to work in the new power plants, or to even *build* them to the necessary specifications... none of that would exist on Earth, and everything would have to be built and taught to us from the ground up.

Thinking that the aliens that visit Earth would be able to come here and build one of their power plants for us would be like us sending ten nuclear scientists and engineers to an island in the middle of the ocean that is inhabited by fifty thousand fishermen and farmers living in rudimentary huts, and asking these ten individuals to use the resources on the island to build a nuclear power plant. Even if uranium existed on the island, building the plant to the necessary specifications would be a huge undertaking with the limited materials and untrained labor available. So, most likely, if the aliens tried to help us, they would need to send a large contingent of their population along with ships full of the necessary equipment and materials to Earth to construct the new energy plants for us. Then they would have to continue to send ships with the necessary materials for resupply, and they would have to stay on Earth for ongoing maintenance. Possibly humans could be trained to maintain some of the equipment, but that is not likely.

I have shared what I know and also what I believe in this book, but over the years, I have heard many other people's beliefs about aliens, and I've read more about them while researching some areas of this book. I know some people say that aliens of a "reptilian" race are here on Earth, and they sometimes assume human form and have evil intentions. That could certainly be true, and nothing would surprise me, but based on my past experiences, I believe that the aliens that have visited me, and most likely the majority if not all of the aliens that visit Earth, are benevolent individuals. I personally believe in "angels" and think that most people believe in them as their lives progress, because of all of the unexplained experiences they have had or have heard from others. I recently read that approximately seventy percent of American adults believe in angels,[4] so if you believe in angels and believe aliens are visiting Earth, then the logical conclusion on how angels are able to intervene and perform miracles is that the aliens are actually our guardian angels. They clearly have very advanced technology and would be able to heal people who are dying from cancer or would be able to lift a car off a person that is trapped beneath it. That is one of the reasons I believe they are benevolent.

Another reason I believe aliens are caring individuals and are concerned about our well-being is the statement they made to me, "Now that you are living in California..." that statement clearly was made to benefit someone. Either it was benefitting me, or some random person in California that I would be there to help or support, or more likely, I was there to support my son. Their statement could certainly have been made for some other reason, but since aliens appear to be filling the role of guardian angels, it makes sense that the statement was made to help someone.

Lastly, I believe that aliens are benevolent based on the way they conduct themselves on Earth. They clearly attempt to stay out of sight the majority of the time. There have certainly been plenty of sightings of their craft flying over Earth, hovering in some spots, and even landing. But overall, they remain out of sight, and when they are spotted, they usually leave quickly. If they had no concerns about whether humans witnessed them or were scared by the sight of them, they would be much more brazen and hovering over cities and other populated areas, because they are undoubtedly curious about us as well. However, some theorize that the aliens have made an agreement with various governments, stating

---

4. Holly Meyer, "Nearly 7 in 10 U.S. adults believe in angels, AP-NORC poll finds," PBS, July 29, 2023, https://www.pbs.org/newshour/nation/
nearly-7-in-10-u-s-adults-believe-in-angels-ap-norc-poll-finds#:~:text=Americans'%20belief%20in%20angels%20(69,higher%20power%20(79%20percent).

that they will attempt to remain hidden as much as possible and limit the number of people that are abducted or experimented on, which would explain their behavior as something other than an act of kindness. But if that that theory is true, and with the capabilities the aliens clearly possess, they would not need to make agreements concerning how they conduct themselves on Earth or with humans unless they desired a peaceful relationship with us.

We do have to wonder, what, if anything, do they want from us? Did they leave us on Earth to create some semblance of civilization that would benefit them in some way, such as so we would be able to help them harvest our minerals, as many people have theorized? But that would indicate that they are not truly benevolent, so I don't believe that theory. Maybe the intention was just to colonize the universe with more intelligent life forms that may or may not be somehow related to them? Or maybe creating humans on Earth was just an experiment for them, and them visiting us is just part of the project. I don't believe that either though, because there are too many events that can't be explained that have happened to humans on Earth now and throughout our history, for which the most logical explanation would be that they were orchestrated by the intelligent life forms that left us here thousands of years ago.

When I was in my late teens and early twenties, I didn't believe in God or any type of life after death, and I hadn't really thought through how my experiences related to what happens to us after we pass on. But once I accepted that my visitors were intelligent life from another planet, and after they told me that they left us here on Earth, I began to find immense comfort in the knowledge that they are watching over us. As I matured and heard and read about other people's experiences, in addition to having more of my own, I came to believe what billions of other people around the world believe: that our souls continue on after our bodies are gone, and that they pass into another state or are reincarnated in another body. I had trouble accepting that in the past because I didn't believe in God, and without a powerful entity such as God, that didn't seem possible. But intelligent life from other planets that has the technology to travel many light-years to Earth and find people such as myself, wherever we are, and communicate with us telepathically could certainly have the capability to take our consciousness, along with our thoughts and memories, from bodies that are no longer living and transfer them into a different state or a new body. That, to me, is logical and at least has some scientific basis. I believe that once everything is revealed to us, we will understand it all, and we will have an incredible existence waiting for us after our physical bodies pass on, one in which our souls are bound to other souls we have been connected to throughout our lives.

APPENDIX: ALIEN ENCOUNTERS DISCUSSION FORUM

O NE REASON I wrote this book was because I was tired of keeping my experiences a secret and I'm sure there are hundreds of thousands if not millions more people around the world that have had experiences they also believe, or know, involve aliens and they are also tired of keeping it a secret and would love to be able to discuss them with someone else. Therefore, I created a website with an online discussion forum that allows people to search for others that have had similar experiences as they have had. It is designed so users can maintain complete anonymity with no emails, names or personal information being shared. You can elect to communicate with others privately or you can share your experiences in a forum setting which is restricted to others that have had alien encounters that helps facilitate more peer support and meaningful comments. It can be found at the link below:

https://www.aliensarewithus.com/
alien-encounters-forum.php

Made in United States
Orlando, FL
09 March 2024

44580378R00055